GET READY

A STUDY IN 1 & 2 THESSALONIANS

BIBLE STUDIES TO IMPACT THE LIVES OF ORDINARY PEOPLE

Written by Marie Dinnen

The Word Worldwide

CHRISTIAN FOCUS

For details of our titles visit us on our website
www.christianfocus.com

ISBN 1-85792-948-9

Copyright © WEC International

Published in 2004 by
Christian Focus Publications, Geanies House,
Fearn, Ross-shire, IV20 ITW, Scotland
and
WEC International, Bulstrode, Oxford Road,
Gerrards Cross, Bucks, SL9 8SZ

Cover design by Alister MacInnes

Printed and bound by J W Arrowsmith, Bristol

CONTENTS

QUESTIONS AND NOTES

ANSWER GUIDE

PREFACE

GEARED FOR GROWTH

'Where there's LIFE there's GROWTH: Where there's GROWTH there's LIFE.'

WHY GROW a study group?

Because as we study the Bible and share together we can

- learn to combat loneliness, depression, staleness, frustration, and other problems
- get to understand and love each other
- become responsive to the Holy Spirit's dealing and obedient to God's Word

and that's GROWTH.

How do you GROW a study group?

- Just start by asking a friend to join you and then aim at expanding your group.
- Study the set portions daily (they are brief and easy: no catches).
- Meet once a week to discuss what you find.
- Befriend others, both Christians and non Christians, and work away together

see how it GROWS!

WHEN you GROW ...

This will happen at school, at home, at work, at play, in your youth group, your student fellowship, women's meetings, mid-week meetings, churches and communities,

you'll be REACHING THROUGH TEACHING

INTRODUCTORY STUDY

Dan:	Were you in the synagogue last Sabbath day, Reuben?
Reuben:	No, Dan, I was in Beroea at that time.
Dan:	You should have heard the man who spoke to us from the Scriptures.
Reuben:	Who was he?
Dan:	A man called Paul, and he had two friends with him – Silas and Timothy. They are from Asia Minor and travel around telling people the most incredible things.
Reuben:	What kind of things?
Dan:	About our Messiah, whom we have been expecting for so long. But you will be able to hear him for yourself. He'll be speaking again next Sabbath.

* * *

Paul:	(reads Isa. 53:3, 7, 8) Dear Jewish brothers, is it not clear to you that our Messiah, who was foretold in this passage, had to suffer and die? The Scriptures show us that he was **not** going to live a life of military power, as so many think, but that He would be despised and even rejected, and would suffer agonizingly and without retaliating.
Reuben:	This doesn't sound like the kind of Messiah we've all been brought up to expect.
Paul:	I agree brother, I agree. But if we had really understood the Scriptures, it would have been clear to us. I myself thought the way you thought for many years but now I see the truth that was there all the time – praise the Lord! The prophets wrote the truth but we have been blind to it for so long. Listen, Isaiah also says (read ch. 50:6). Yes, God told us plainly that His Holy One would have to suffer.
Aristarchus:	But all men suffer and all men die. Surely God's Chosen One would be different and would accomplish great things. God will show us by some miraculous happening when His Messiah appears.
Dan:	Messiah will never die! It is written in the Psalms that God will not leave Him in the place of the dead, nor will His body decay. Messiah will never die!
Paul:	You're right, brother, in saying that the Christ would not **stay** in the place of the dead, nor would His body decay but don't you see, that didn't mean that He wouldn't die; it meant that He would rise from the dead!

Secundus:	Rise from the dead?
Damas:	Rise from the dead! What nonsense! I'm a Greek, and I concede that the soul is immortal, but not the body.
Secundus:	I'm interested. I'd like to hear more. Surely only God could rise from the dead.
Paul:	And is not Messiah God's Chosen One? Is it strange that God Himself should be able to raise the dead?
Aristarchus:	Well, when Messiah comes we'll see. If He does have to suffer and die, as the Scriptures seem to say, all right. But I will only be convinced of his identity when He does rise from the dead!
Paul:	My friend, He already has.
Aristarchus:	Has what?
Dan:	Risen from the dead?
Secundus:	What is this man saying?
Paul:	Dear brother Jews, this is the tremendous news I bring you. Our Messiah has come. He came to His own people, the Jews, but they despised and rejected Him. He has suffered more than any man has suffered. He was ... crucified ... at the hands of cruel men. But He arose from the dead and is alive for evermore. His name Jesus of Nazareth, God's Son, the Christ.
Reuben:	Where is He, then? Is He still in Jerusalem?
Paul:	My friends, He is now seated at the right hand of God, in all power and glory.
Demas:	I knew there was a catch. How do we know that what you say is true?
Paul:	The Holy Spirit will speak to your hearts to show you the truth. There was a time when I hardened my heart against this teaching and even (*softly*) persecuted His followers. But our Lord Jesus, in His mercy, met me yes, I even saw Him at the Father's right hand, so that I would be equipped to pass this wonderful news on to others. This Jesus, whom I proclaim to you, is the Christ, the Messiah.
Secundus:	This is the truth! I believe it.
Aristarchus:	I too. What joy this brings to my soul!
Demas:	Well, I think it is false teaching. I will not stay any longer.
Jason:	Paul, we would hear more of this but the hour of worship is at an end. My name is Jason. Come with us to my house where we can talk further.
Secundus:	Yes, let us know more. I am a Greek. Believing in Jesus brings peace and satisfaction such as our idols never brought. Surely your God is the living and true God.
Paul:	Dear brothers, Silas, Timothy and I are available to you at any time of the day or night. We work at our tent-making whenever we can, but this is only secondary to telling you people about the wonderful good news of Jesus

Christ. It is joy unspeakable to preach the Gospel! Thank you, Jason, we shall go to your house.

* * *

Silas:	Well, Paul, what wonderful opportunities we have here in Thessalonica, and how receptive the people are.
Paul:	Yes, Silas. The Lord is good. We have been almost a month here now, and still people come daily to learn more of the faith.
Timothy:	Have you noticed that there are more Greeks accepting the Lord than Jews?
Silas:	Yes, these men have really been searching for reality, and now they have found it in Jesus.
Timothy:	The Jews have been steeped in their tradition too long. Their hearts are hardened. All through history the Jews have persecuted God's prophets.
Paul:	Timothy, **I know**. Yet God is so gracious, and He can soften the hardest heart. **I know.**
Silas:	It thrills me to see a good number of the leading women of the city among our converts, too. Surely the Lord is going to build a strong church here.
Paul:	Listen! What is that noise? It is some kind of riot.
Jason:	Paul! Silas! Timothy! Hide yourselves, quickly. Down through the back of the house and out by the way of the lane. There's no time to lose!
Silas:	What's happening?
Jason:	The city is in an uproar. The Jews are jealous of you, as so many people are becoming Christians. The Jews know you are here and have gathered a crowd of rough fellows who are coming to attack the house.
Paul:	What about you, brother?
Jason:	Don't worry about me. Can't I suffer, too, for the name of our precious Lord? Now, off you go, quickly!
X.	(*hammering at the door*) Let us in! Let us in!
Jason:	What do you want, friends?
Y:	Where are they? **Those Christians**. Paul and the others.
X:	Come on, boys, don't ask him, he's one of them. We're going to ferret them out. Get out of the way.
Y:	They're probably hiding somewhere. Hey, you **Christians**, come out. We'll get you.
X:	They don't seem to be here.
Y:	Those Jews did say Jason's house, didn't they?
X:	I've looked everywhere. They're definitely not in the house.

Y:	Well, if we can't find them, we'll take Jason and some others. Come on, drag him out.
X:	Bring them along to the city authorities, they'll know what to do with them.
City man:	What on earth is going on? Who are these men?
Jew 1:	These are lawless citizens. They have been harbouring troublemakers. This one, Jason, has had them staying at his house.
City man:	And who are these troublemakers?
Jew 2:	Three men, called Paul, Silas and Timothy. We've heard of them at Philippi. They were put in jail there.
Jew 1:	They have turned the world upside down wherever they have gone, disturbing the peace and breaking the law and now they have come here.
City man:	Why, what do they do? What do they speak about?
Jew 2:	They act against the decrees of Caesar. They say people must worship another king, called Jesus.
City man:	This is serious. This is very serious indeed. And you can't find these men?
Jew 1:	No, but Jason has had them staying at his house.
City man:	Then Jason must be responsible for them. He must go bail for them. The matter is settled. We don't want any more riots or lawbreaking in a respectable city like Thessalonica.

* * *

Jason:	Paul? Is that you in the shadows? It is I, Jason.
Paul:	Dear brother. You have been suffering in our place. If only we could have spared you.
Jason:	Brother Paul, we are but following in our Master's steps, as He suffered for us. But now, dear friends, you must leave our city this very night, as I fear you could no longer preach openly.
Timothy:	It is as the Lord wills. It must be His plan for us to move on to the next place.
Silas:	May God give you and our other brothers in Christ strength to stand fast in the Lord, even in the face of great opposition.
Paul:	We will go then, Jason. Don't be surprised if you hear that we are persecuted in every city where we proclaim that Jesus is the Christ. Suffering is bound to continue, but we can rejoice that God counts us worthy to suffer for His sake. The Lord will reward you for your hospitality and love to us. We will journey south, and will return as soon as He allows us. Peace be to you in the name of our Lord Jesus Christ.

STUDY 1

THE MARKS OF A CHRISTIAN

QUESTIONS

DAY 1 *1 Thessalonians 1:1; 1 Corinthians 1:2.*
a) What does Paul mean when he writes 'the church'?

b) What is the relationship of the Christian to God the Father and the Lord Jesus Christ?

DAY 2 *1 Thessalonians 1:2-3; 1 Corinthians 13:1-13.*
a) What three things about the Thessalonian Christians did Paul always remember to thank God for?

b) What does 1 Corinthians 13:13 tell us about these three graces?

DAY 3 *1 Thessalonians 1:4-5; John 17:6; Ephesians 1:3-4.*
a) What is Paul so certain about in verse 4?

b) For what purpose does God do this?

DAY 4 *1 Thessalonains 1:5-7.*
a) Whose example did the believers at Thessalonica follow?

QUESTIONS (contd.)

b) How did the Lord use them as they followed Him?

c) What can we learn from these verses?

DAY 5   *I Thessalonians 1:5-8.*
Read the play, 'Paul in Thessalonica' through again. Can you see that the gospel came in power and in the Holy Spirit? Notice that they received the word with full conviction (v. 5) and with much affliction (v. 6).

DAY 6   *I Thessalonians 1:9-10.*
Compare verse 3 with these verses. Can you find a parallel here with faith? love? hope?

DAY 7   *I Thessalonians 1:1-10.*
a) List the marks of a Christian, as shown in this chapter.

b) Does the description fit you? If not, what are you going to do about it?

NOTES

The Christian life is 3-dimensional. Faith gives it depth, hope gives it length and love gives it breadth.

Look up the following references and notice how faith (trust), hope (looking forward) and love are thought of together.

I Thessalonians 5:8
Romans 5:1-5
Galatians 5:5, 6 (expressed differently in LB)
Colossians 1:4, 5
Hebrews 10:22-24
I Peter 1:21, 22

These are three essentials of our Christian life, so let us make quite sure we know exactly what the words mean.

FAITH

We might say that the one, overruling message of the New Testament is that there is only one way to become part of God's family and have everlasting life and that is **by faith** in His Son, Jesus.

Romans 5:1 tells us that we are 'justified' (or made right with God) only **by faith**, and this is how we can get peace with God. If you are still looking for that inner peace, which you perhaps envy in other people, then read the following quotation carefully.

'Central to the New Testament is the thought that God sent His Son to be the Saviour of the World. Christ accomplished man's salvation by dying an atoning death on Calvary's cross. FAITH is the attitude whereby **a man abandons all reliance in his own efforts to obtain salvation**, be they deeds of piety, of ethical goodness, or anything else. It is the attitude of complete trust in Christ, of reliance on Him alone for all that salvation means.' (New Bible Dictionary)

Faith is not merely intellectual assent to certain truths ('the devils also believe, and tremble', Jas. 2:19); it is believing unreservedly that the best life we can live is just not good enough and God will only accept us when we have accepted Christ.

HOPE

The important thing to realize is that **Christian hope is certainty**. We often use the word 'hope' in exactly the opposite way, because we are doubtful if something will happen.

We say 'I hope it will'.

Why is the hope that the Bible talks about, a certainty?

'O Israel, hope in the Lord' (Ps. 130:7)
'Blessed is the man ... whose hope the Lord is' (Jer. 17:7)
'Christ Jesus, our hope' (I Tim. 1:1)

Those who have 'no hope' are described as being 'without God' (Eph. 2:12). You will see that 'all our hope on God is founded' and this is why it is sure, steadfast, immovable, an anchor of the soul.

LOVE

Ask ten different people for a definition of love, and they will give you ten different answers. The Bible tells us,

'God is Love'
'God so loved ... that He **gave** His Son'

Although the study of the word LOVE could occupy a whole term, let us sum it up in two words : SELF-GIVING.

'The utter disregard of self in the service of God and man is what the Bible calls LOVE' (John Stott).

Jesus said, 'This is my commandment, that you LOVE one another' ...

Think about it.

STUDY 2

THE LIFE OF A CHRISTIAN WORKER

QUESTIONS

DAY 1 *1 Thessalonians 2 (whole chapter); 2:10; 2 Peter 3:10-12.*
Was Paul living the kind of life suggested by Peter, as he waited for the return of Christ?

DAY 2 *1 Thessalonians 2:1,2; Acts 16:19-24.*
a) What exactly happened to Paul and Silas at Philippi?

b) After all this, how did they dare to go and preach the same message in the next town?

DAY 3 *1 Thessalonians 2:3-6; 2 Corinthians 5:9; Hebrews 11:5.*
a) How does Paul make it quite clear that the message he proclaimed originated with God?

b) What do these verses show should be the whole aim of a Christian's life?

DAY 4 *1 Thessalonians 2:7-12; 4:1; 5:14-18.*
a) What was Paul's attitude to those he worked amongst?

b) What did he exhort and encourage them to do?

QUESTIONS (contd.)

DAY 5 *1 Thessalonians 2:13-16; Acts 7:51,52; John 1:11.*
a) What was another reason for Paul to give thanks?

b) How were the Thessalonian Christians like the Christians in Judea? Can you see how they were all like their Master in this?

DAY 6 *1 Thessalonians 2:17-20; Ephesians 6:12.*
a) To what does Paul attribute the fact that he was not able to visit his friends in Thessalonica?

b) As well as seeing the Lord Jesus when He returns, what else is Paul looking forward to?

DAY 7 *1 Thessalonians 2:2, 8, 19.*
a) There they are again! Faith, hope and love. Which verse fits which?

b) These verses show the practical outworking of faith, hope and love. Can you share with the group how they work out in your life?

NOTES

'Our message to you is true, our motives are pure, our conduct is absolutely above board. We speak under the solemn sense of being entrusted by God with the gospel' (I Thess. 2:3, Phillips).

* * *

A legend is told relating to the time when Jesus ascended to heaven. It is said that He was greeted in the glory by tens of thousands of angels and archangels, who put the question to Him – 'Mighty Lord of all Creation, you have spent three short years on earth preaching about the Kingdom and have now returned to heaven; what provision have you made for spreading the gospel to those who do not have eternal life?'

To this Jesus replied, 'I have Peter, James, John and the others who have been with me. They will spread the Good News around the world!'

There was a horrified silence. Then one angel voiced the thoughts of all the others. 'Master' he said, 'these men are human! They are only a handful. They are weak and unreliable. What other plan will you put into action if they fail you?'

Jesus said, 'I have no other plan. I am depending on them.'

* * *

On whom does Jesus depend today for the spreading of His word? If you had a friend who had cancer and you heard that a cure had been discovered, would you keep that good news to yourself? Yet many around you are 'spiritually dead and doomed by their sins' (Eph. 2:5), 'having no hope and without God' (Eph. 2:12).

With your group, discuss what practical ways **you** can be available for God to use.

'Take my life and let it be
consecrated, Lord to Thee.
Take my moments and my days,
let them flow in ceaseless praise.'

Take my hands ... my feet ... my voice ... my lips ... my silver and my gold ... my intellect ... my will ... my heart ... my love ... myself.

STUDY 3

PRAYING EARNESTLY

QUESTIONS

DAY 1   *1 Thessalonians 3:10; 1:2; 5:17.*
a) These are key verses in this letter. What was the secret of Paul's effective ministry?

b) Read Romans 8:26. Do you ever feel you don't know how to pray? How does this verse help us?

DAY 2   *1 Thessalonians 3:1-5; Acts 14:21, 22.*
a) What was it that Paul could not bear any longer? What did he do about it?

b) What warning did he usually bring when revisiting new converts?

DAY 3   *Acts 18:5; 1 Thessalonians 3:6-8.*
a) What was the good news that Timothy brought?

b) Can you think of one person you have spoken to about Jesus, and prayed for? (A friend, neighbour, relative, one of your own children, child in a Sunday School class, etc.) Is this person 'standing fast in the Lord'?

QUESTIONS (contd.)

DAY 4 *I Thessalonians 1:3, 9; 2:7, 8, 17; 3:6.*

a) From these verses (and others that we have read), can you get some idea of the deep feeling of love Paul had for these brothers in the Lord?

b) Think of your own church fellowship. Are you satisfied that this kind of love is being shown amongst your brothers and sisters in Christ? Read John 15:12. Note down any steps you can take to do this better.

DAY 5 *I Thessalonians 3:9, 10; Philippians 4:6.*

a) How did Paul pray for these people?

b) Be honest and specific about this question: Do you pray regularly?

DAY 6 *I Thessalonians 3:11-13; Ephesians 1:4.*

a) What requests does Paul make in this prayer for his friends?

b) Why is holiness the aim of the Christian? (v. 13)

As you pray for someone this week, use the words of verses 12 and 13.

DAY 7 *John 17*

a) Read carefully this great prayer of Jesus. For whom is He praying (vv. 9, 20)?

b) What requests does He make on behalf of these people?

NOTES

'Of course, Paul, you were an **experienced** Christian, so I suppose prayer came easily to you. You didn't have children to look after, or a home to run, and you didn't live in our pressurized 21st Century, so I suppose you had more time....'

'Wait a minute! How does a Christian become an "experienced" Christian? I had to begin at the beginning too, you know. But my greatest desire was that I might know Jesus Christ better and the best way to get to know a person is to talk to him often, about everything, and to be with him as much as possible. Do you agree?'

'Yes. I see your point. Undoubtedly that's the best way to get to know someone.'

'True, I didn't live in the 21st Century, but there were only 24 hours in each day in the 1st Century too! You can read about how hard I worked, how I was put in jail frequently, how I faced death again and again. I was beaten with rods, stoned, shipwrecked three times. I travelled many weary miles and have been through many kinds of danger. I have lived with weariness, pain and sleepless nights; I have often been hungry and thirsty and have gone without food; often been shivering with cold, without enough clothing to keep me warm. Besides all this, I had the constant worry of how all the churches were getting on (2 Cor. 11:23-27).

'Children? I talked to my converts as a father to his own children don't you remember? – pleading with them, encouraging them and even demanding that their lives should bring joy and glory to God (1 Thess. 2:11, 12). Some were only baby Christians and these I had to feed with milk and not solid food, because they couldn't digest anything stronger (1 Cor. 3:2, 3). How gentle I had to be with them, like a nurse taking care of her children!'

'Sorry, Paul, I take back all I said. I've got no excuse at all. Can you give us, from the chapter we've been reading this week, some pointers to help us when we pray for someone?'

'With pleasure. Here you are –

(a) Be earnest about the person you are praying for (v. 10)
(b) Keep in touch with that person, no matter how difficult it may seem (v. 2)
(c) Thank God for every encouragement, every answer to your prayers (v. 9)
(d) Pray regularly (v. 10)
(e) Don't be afraid to tell the person you are praying for them (v. 10)
(f) Expect God to work. He is stronger than Satan, and can make the impossible possible (v. 11, cf. 2:18)
(g) Pray specifically (v. 12, 13)'

'Well, that's great. This list will surely help us to pray earnestly for others.'

STUDY 4

HOLINESS – WITHOUT WHICH NO ONE WILL SEE THE LORD

QUESTIONS

DAY 1   *1 Thessalonians 3:13–4:8.*
a) How many times in these verses can you find the words 'holy' and 'holiness'?

b) Did you spot the word 'holy' in verse 8? How does God equip each one of us for holy living?

DAY 2   *1 Peter 1:13-16.*
a) Why is it important that our standards for personal holiness are high?

b) 1 John 1:8-10. In what practical way can you daily become holy?

DAY 3   *1 Thessalonians 4:1,2.*
Read these verses carefully, in several versions if possible. What do you learn from them? What kind of things should we be doing more and more?

DAY 4   *1 Thessalonians 4:2-6; Matthew 5:28.*
What is the theme of this passage? Be prepared to discuss how we can help our children, teenagers, friends, or young people we meet to live up to God's standards set out here.

QUESTIONS (contd.)

DAY 5 *1 Thessalonians 4:6-8.*
a) What reason is given here for guarding against sexual sin?

b) If we disobey the moral standards in the Bible, who are we despising?

DAY 6 *1 Thessalonians 4:9-12.*
a) Look back to the section on Love in Study 1, and Day 4 in last week's questions. What does verse 10 tell us to do?

b) Why are Christians urged to live quietly and do their own work?

DAY 7 *2 Peter 3:10-12; Hebrews 12:14; Romans 13:11-14.*
a) What do these three readings urge us to do?

b) What reason do Peter and Paul both give for the necessity to live a holy and disciplined life?

NOTES

'Strive for holiness.' RSV
'Seek to live a clean and holy life.' LB
'Aim at a holy life.' NEB
'Let it be your ambition to achieve holiness.' Phillips.

The first condition of living a holy life is that we **want** to live a holy life. It's as simple as that. How much we achieve holiness is in direct proportion to how much we desire it.

How much do you long to be holy? i.e., set apart for God to use. Holiness is not an unattainable ideal reserved for the few, it is what God expects of every child of His.

Has He spoken to you this week about anything He wants you to put right in your life?

Holiness is God giving you a clean sheet when you confess and put away something that is wrong.

You may like to use this hymn as a prayer:

> O my Father, take me, make me
> Pure and holy, all Thine own;
> May each changing moment find me
> At Thy footstool, near Thy throne.
>
> Oh, my Saviour, cleanse me, fill me
> With Thy precious love divine,
> May no earthly idol turn me
> From that sacred Cross of Thine.
>
> Holy Spirit, woo me, draw me
> By Thy gentle cords of love;
> Guide me, guard me, safely lead me
> To my heavenly home above.

HINDRANCES TO HOLINESS

Bitterness (Heb. 12:15).
Immorality (Heb. 12:16).
Love of money (Heb. 13:5).
Lack of love for others.

HELPS TO HOLINESS

Prayer: regular and specific.
Bible Study: disciplined and approached intelligently.
Fellowship meeting with other Christians for worship.
Service to others.
Keeping our eyes on Jesus always.

Can you match up the list of 'helps' with the hymn below?

Take time to be holy,
Speak oft with Thy Lord,
Abide in Him always
And feed on His Word.
Make friends of God's children,
Help those who are weak,
Forgetting in nothing
His blessing to seek.

Take time to be holy,
The world rushes on,
Spend much time in secret
With Jesus alone.
By looking to Jesus
Like Him thou shalt be,
Thy friends, in thy conduct,
His likeness shall see.

STUDY 5

A COMFORTING HOPE

QUESTIONS

DAY 1   *1 Thessalonians 4:13-18.*
a) Why would these verses have been a comforting hope to those who first read them?

b) Are they still a comfort to us today?

DAY 2   *1 Thessalonians 4:13; 1 Corinthians 15:17-23.*
a) Why does the Bible say Christians should not grieve like others when another Christian dies?

b) How are unbelievers described here?

DAY 3   *1 Thessalonians 4:14; 1 Corinthians 15:35-50.*
a) What makes it possible to believe that those who die will be raised at the return of Christ?

b) What illustration is given to show the difference between the physical body and the spiritual body?

DAY 4   *1 Thessalonians 4:15; 2:13; John 14:1-6.*
a) How would you answer a person who found it hard to believe the passage in Thessalonians we are studying this week.?

b) Does verse 15 show any advantage to Christians who are still alive when Christ returns?

DAY 5 *1 Thessalonians 4:15, 17; John 5:28, 29; Matthew 24:30, 31.*
a) Who is the central figure in the drama foretold here?

b) What is the ultimate blessing to which we look forward as believers?

DAY 6 *1 Thessalonians 4:18; 1 Corinthians 15:51-58.*
a) How can this week's study help us in our daily life?

b) What have you learned from it?

DAY 7 *1 Thessalonians 4:13-18; Revelation 20:11–21:5.*
a) What solemn warning can you find in the reading from Revelation?

b) How is eternal life in God's presence described?

NOTES

Have you ever waited at an airport for someone you love very much to arrive? One of the family who has been away for some time: a sister or parent whom you haven't seen for years, a fiancee you've been separated from for at least two weeks!

Stop reading for a moment, and think how you felt.

Perhaps you got to the airport early and have waited endlessly, it seems, and now the moment is here. Perhaps it was 'one of those days' and problems and difficulties all but prevented you getting there, but those things are forgotten as the time of arrival approaches.

Peter writes: 'Look eagerly for the coming of the Day of God, and work to hasten it on' (2 Pet. 3:12 NEB) .

The Thessalonian believers had learned from Paul that Jesus Christ would come again, in the same way as His disciples had seen Him go at the ascension (Acts 1:9-11) less than 20 years before. They expected Him to return in their lifetime, so when some of the Christians died, the others became worried in case they had missed out on the anticipated 'Royal Visit' (the meaning of the word used to denote the return of Christ).

Some may even have thought Paul was mistaken.

So Paul writes these verses to dispel their fears and encourage them to continue to wait expectantly. He describes The Royal Visit in terms we can all understand, borrowing his imagery from the pageantry of Greek rulers when they arrived in triumph. The shout, the voice and the trumpet were to herald the arrival of the King, giving drama and excitement to the event – but how much more dramatic and exciting will be the coming of our Lord Jesus Christ, when we shall see Him face to face and go to be with Him forever.

Many views and theories are put forward today to discredit the teaching of a personal return of Jesus Christ. Let us not be influenced by them. We should read and re-read the straightforward record of the New Testament writers so that we shall not be led astray by sophisticated speculations. Only thus shall we have the peace and assurance of the comforting hope about which we have been thinking this week.

STUDY 6

WAKE UP! WATCH! WAIT ...

QUESTIONS

DAY 1   *I Thessalonians 5:1-3; Matthew 24:42-44; Revelation 3:3.*
a) Why do you think the day of the Lord is likened to a thief in the night?

b) What command does Jesus give about this?

DAY 2   *I Thessalonians 5:4-8; Ephesians 5:8-14.*
a) Make 2 lists to show the contrast between light and darkness.

b) What 3 Christian characteristics can you find in I Thessalonians 5:8?

DAY 3   *I Thessalonians 5:9-11; 2 Peter 3:8-10.*
a) What does God wish for every man?

b) Why did Christ die for us?

DAY 4   *I Thessalonians 5:12-15.*
a) Can you see any connection between this section and the beginning of the chapter?

QUESTIONS (contd.)

b) Two of these verses are written to the layman, and one particularly to Church leaders. Can you spot them?

DAY 5 *I Thessalonians 5:16-22.*
a) Pick out and list the positive commands and the negative ones.

b) With verse 18, read Philippians 4:6. How far do you carry out this will of God for you?

DAY 6 *I Thessalonians 5:23-28.*
a) Compare verse 23 with chapter 3:13. Are you remembering to pray for people in this way?

b) What request does Paul make to his readers? Do you remember to pray for the leaders in your church?

DAY 7 *2 Peter 3:11-18.*
a) What does Peter urge us to do during this waiting time?

b) Wake up! Watch! Wait ... Do you see how these words apply to the New Testament teaching on the return of Christ? (see notes)?

NOTES

WAKE UP! to the facts!

Christ left His people with a sure promise that He would return. Did you know that in the 260 chapters of the New Testament our Lord's coming again is mentioned 318 times? The familiar words of Jesus in John 14, 'I will come again' are hallowed by sacred sentiment. Have you thought seriously about what difference it will make to you personally when He returns? And with so many people's lives being cut short these days with accident or disease, how can we know how much time we have, even if we die before He comes?

So 'wake up, for the coming of the Lord is nearer now than when we first believed' (Rom. 13:11 LB).

WATCH!

When Jesus told His disciples that His coming would be like lightning and like a thief in the night, He was showing them that it would be sudden. No time to give your life to Him if you haven't done that before. No time to put things right, to say 'sorry' to someone, to speak to a friend about Him – no time! So Jesus added, 'Watch, therefore, for you do not know on what day your Lord is coming.' His coming will be unexpected to many, but Christians should not be caught by surprise. 'Watch, therefore.'

WAIT ... in an attitude of joyous expectancy.

Just think – 'When He appears, we shall be like Him, for we shall see Him as He is' (1 John 3:2). But this waiting time is a time for preparation.

Are you ready to meet Jesus if He should come tonight?

Do you know Him as your Saviour and Lord? Then learn to know Him more and more.

Do you love His word? Then study it more and more. Are you obeying His command to love others? Then do so more and more.

STUDY 7

THE OTHER SIDE OF THE COIN

QUESTIONS

This second letter was written as soon as Paul heard how his first letter had been received and contains further teaching about the Lord's return.

DAY 1   *2 Thessalonians 1:1-4; Acts 17:5-9, 13.*
a) From whom would the persecution have come?

b) What does Paul notice about the Thessalonian Christians in spite of their trials and hardships?

DAY 2   *2 Thessalonians 1:5-7; 1 Peter 3:13-17.*
a) Can you find here any reasons why God allows His children to endure suffering?

b) When Christians are persecuted for their faith, what lies ahead for their persecutors?

DAY 3   *2 Thessalonians 1:6-9.*
a) What kind of people will come under God's judgment when Jesus returns?

b) How can you reconcile v. 9 with God's character?

QUESTIONS (contd.)

DAY 4 *Matthew 13:24-30, 36-43, 47-50.*
a) How will the coming of Christ have two devastatingly different results?

b) What verse in today's reading is similar to 2 Thessalonians 1:7 ?

DAY 5 *Matthew 25:1-13; 31-46.*
a) What warning is there for us in the parable of the ten virgins?

b) In Christ's pictorial description of the judgment scene, do we find any suggestion of a second chance?

DAY 6 *2 Thessalonians 1:9, 10; Revelation 1:7; 22:12.*
a) What fact stands out from these verses as bring absolutely certain?

b) How is the punishment described for those who refuse to ac knowledge Jesus Christ?

DAY 7 *2 Thessalonians 1:11, 12.*
a) What is Paul's prayer for his friends? Put it in your own words.

b) Read through the whole of chapter 1 again to find out why he prays this for them.

NOTES

In that wonderfully graphic passage in I Thessalonians 4:15-17 we read about the joyous expectation of the Christian. When Christ returns, it will be a time of bliss and blessing for His people. The Bible makes it very clear that it is those who are in Christ who can look forward to being **with Christ** at His coming.

But this implies that there is another side to the coin.

What of those who are not **in Christ**? What awaits those who will not be taken to be **with Christ**? As we saw in our study this week, they will suffer the punishment of being cut off from the presence of the Lord. Can you imagine being cut off from EVERYTHING that is good, pure or true?

The penalty for choosing to live without God in this life is that we shall be compelled to live without Him in the next.

* * *

The Old Testament prophets foretold the day of judgment, e.g.,

Enoch	'Behold, the Lord came with His myriads, to execute judgment' (Jude 14).
Isaiah	'The Lord of Hosts has a day against all that is proud and lofty ... and the Lord alone will be exalted in that day' (Isa. 2:12 and 17).
Psalmist	'He comes to judge the earth. He will judge the world with righteousness' (Ps. 98:9).
Malachi	'The Lord, whom you seek, will suddenly come to His temple ... but who can endure the day of His coming, and who can stand when He appears?' (Mal. 3:1 and 2).

The New Testament, as we have seen this week, has many references to it, e.g.,

Jesus	'He who hears my words and believes Him who has sent me, has eternal life, he does not come into judgment' (John 5:24).
	'He (Jesus) is the one ordained by God to be the judge of the living and the dead' (Acts 10:42).
Paul	'He has fixed a day on which he will judge the world in righteousness' (Acts 17:31).
James	'There is one lawgiver and judge, He who is able to save and to destroy' (Jas. 4:12).
The writer to the Hebrews.	'It is appointed for men to die once, and after that comes judgment' (Heb. 9:27).

The early Christian creeds affirm it, and show that it has always been a basic essential of our faith.

'From thence He (Jesus) shall come to judge the quick and the dead' (The Apostles' Creed, and Nicene Creed).
'At whose coming all men shall rise again with their bodies, and shall give account for their own works. And they that have done good shall go into life everlasting: and they that have done evil into everlasting fire' (Athanasius' Creed).
'We believe that Thou shalt come to be our judge' (Te Deum).

* * *

Notice, however, this interesting point about salvation and judgment: When God speaks of salvation, He underlines it with the certainty of judgment. And when He speaks of judgment, at the same time He offers salvation to all who will come.

e.g., John 3:18: 'He who believes in Him is not condemned; he who does not believe is condemned already, because he has not believed in the name of the only Son of God.'

As God looks at our world today, He sees two kinds of people those who love Him and those who do not love Him. We cannot see into men's hearts, so often it is not possible for us to distinguish one from the other. When the Lord Jesus is 'revealed' (see v. 9 of our study chapter) at His return, the hearts of men will also be revealed. So His coming will have a dual purpose: to vindicate His own people and to punish those who have chosen to ignore or reject Him.

STUDY 8

QUESTIONS

DAY 1 *2 Thessalonians 2:1, 2; 3:11, 12.*
a) What wrong teaching had been rumoured among some of the Thessalonian Christians?

b) What had Paul heard that some people were doing?

DAY 2 *2 Thessalonians 2:3-5.*
a) What two things will happen before Jesus comes again?

b) What will the man of lawlessness (man of sin, or man of rebellion) do when he is revealed?

DAY 3 *2 Thessalonians 2:6-12; 2 Timothy 3:1-5; 2 Timothy 4:3-4.*
a) Why has this agent of Satan not yet been revealed, although his work is going on?

b) What will happen to the wicked one when Christ appears?

DAY 4 *2 Thessalonians 2:6-12 (again); 1 Timothy 4:1, 2, 7, 8.*
a) What kind of things will the man of lawlessness demonstrate when he comes?

QUESTIONS (contd.)

b) Who are the people who will be deceived by the lies of this man?

DAY 5 *Matthew 24:10-13; Revelation 12:7-12.*
a) How are the devil and his agents described in these passages?

b) What great and glorious assurance comes through for those who belong to Christ?

DAY 6 *2 Thessalonians 2:13-15; I Thessalonians 1:4.*
a) What 2 encouragements for believers are repeated in these verses?

b) Paul gives 2 important pieces of advice. What are they?

DAY 7 *2 Thessalonians 2:16, 17; I Thessalonians 3:11-13; 2 Corinthians 13:14.*
a) In this first prayer, what does Paul say God has done for us?

b) What petitions does Paul make for believers?

NOTES

What a pity we can't go back in time.

Then we could drop in to Thessalonica and hear what exactly Paul was saying as he taught the people there.

Isn't it tantalizing to read –

'Don't you remember what I told you ... (v. 5)
... about the coming of our Lord Jesus Christ? (v. 1)
... about our assembling to meet Him? (v. 1)
... about the rebellion? (v. 3)
... about the man of lawlessness? (v. 3)'
and, 'You know what is restraining him ...' (v. 6)

* * *

Second Thessalonians 2 is acknowledged to be one of the most difficult passages in the Bible to interpret. Many people speculate on the exact meaning of the words and link them up with other passages to their own satisfaction, but Dr Leon Morris in the *Tyndale commentary,* after deep study, has come to the conclusion that:

'It is well for us to bear in mind that we do not possess the key to everything that is here said, and accordingly to maintain some reserve in our interpretations.'

Who is the man of lawlessness?
Has he already appeared in history?
Shall we see a world dictator arise to fulfil the role?
Will Communism produce such a man?
Can we find any clues to his identity?
These are tempting questions, but God's Word gives us no clear-cut answers.

John writes in his epistle,

'Children, it is the last hour; and as you have heard that Antichrist is coming, so now many antichrists have come; therefore we know that it is the last hour.'

From time to time we must expect that outstandingly evil men will appear. Yet Paul is writing here about the most infamous of them all, who will be revealed when the end is near. This should warn us of the existence of an enemy strong and powerful – that old Serpent, the devil. And he is not dead yet, though he would like us to think so!

The man of lawlessness is the man of sin, and sin, by definition, is rebellion against God.
'The mystery of lawlessness' (v. 7) is man setting himself up as God.
'The mystery of godliness' (I Tim. 3:16) is God becoming man. It is with a sense of relief that Paul turns from the gloom of writing about evil and the fate of those who refuse to believe the truth, to the brightness of a future full of hope and comfort for the believer.
What a joy to know what it is to be loved with everlasting love!

'His for ever, only His:
Who the Lord and me shall part?
Ah, with what a rest of bliss
Christ can fill the loving heart.
Heaven and earth may fade and flee,
First-born light in gloom decline;
But, while God and I shall be,
I am His, and He is mine.'

STUDY 9

QUESTIONS

DAY 1 Think back over these two letters written by Paul. Look again at the studies we have done this term, the questions, the notes.
What stands out most in your mind?

What challenge have you felt, and what are you doing about it?

DAY 2 *2 Peter 3:3-10; Ephesians 5:16.*
a) How would you explain the fact that Christians in every age have thought that the Lord's coming was imminent, and yet He hasn't yet come?

b) What are we urged to be doing as we wait for Him?

DAY 3 *2 Thessalonians 3:1, 2; Acts 17:5, 13; Acts 18:12.*
a) What is one thing we still have opportunity to do while the Lord delays His coming?

b) What prayer requests did Paul make? Do you remember to pray for your minister, that he might faithfully preach the Lord's message?

DAY 4 *2 Thessalonians 3:3-5; 2 Timothy 1:12.*
a) Note another opportunity which presents itself as we wait for the Lord.

QUESTIONS (contd.)

b) Why can we look to the future with confidence?

DAY 5 *2 Thessalonians 3:6, 14, 15.*
a) Try to envisage the situation Paul is writing about. Why do you think he commanded Christians to hold themselves aloof from other Christians who refused to work?

b) What action can be taken towards those who disobey? Helping those who fall is another opportunity we still have.

DAY 6 *2 Thessalonians 3:7-13; Exodus 20:9; John 5:17.*
a) Apply this passage to your daily life. What other opportunity do we have day by day before He comes again?

b) What do you think would be the benefits of this practical advice to the believers at Thessalonica?

DAY 7 *2 Thessalonians 3:16-18; Romans 5:1; Philippians 4:7; John 14:27.*
a) What are the two kinds of peace the Bible speaks about?

b) Look back to 1 Thessalonians 1:1. Paul ends his letters the way he began, by praying for two precious gifts for his friends. What are they? Do you have them?

NOTES

Samuel Beckett wrote a cynical and excessively dull play called 'Waiting for Godot'. It has virtually no plot.

Two disgusting, dirty tramps wait under a tree. They wait day after day, year after year – for what? Anything to relieve them of the intolerable burden of existence, the agony of making a decision. They can no longer act, they can only wait, wait for someone else to do the work for them, to take the initiative, wait for a symbolic character who promises but never comes, named Godot.

The play ends with these lines,

'We'll hang ourselves tomorrow unless Godot comes.'
'And if he comes?'
'We'll be saved. Well, shall we go?'
'Yes, let's go.'
      But they do not move a step.

* * *

The unbeliever (if he thinks about it at all) sees the Christian as a gullible fool waiting for God-ot, a little god, who is not really there and who certainly will never come to the rescue of his feeble followers.

Is this the impression the Bible gives of our great, almighty Creator God who is the source of all power and riches and wisdom and strength and honour and glory and blessing? Far from it.

What an exciting experience it is to live day by day in thrilling anticipation! The time will come when our Lord Jesus Christ will fulfil the promise that He gave when He said, 'I will come again'.

What sort of lives should we be living? What golden opportunities do we have now, in this intervening time before He comes?

The opportunity to pray for others,
to spread God's word,
to put into practice the things we are learning from our studies,
to help others who are weak in the faith,
to make the most of the time and not be idle.

Just think:

When Jesus returns, it will be too late to help another to find salvation, to share with others what Christ means to you, too late to say that word of encouragement or cheer – too late! Do it now, while there is time.

God's Word tingles with excitement as it beckons us to look ahead to that glorious day when those who love Jesus will see Him as He is. Listen!

'They will see the Son of Man coming on the clouds of heaven with power and great glory' (Matt. 24:30).

'This Jesus, who was taken from you into heaven, will come in the same way as you saw Him go into heaven' (Acts 1:11).

'The Lord Himself will descend from heaven with a cry of command, with the archangel's call, and with the sound of the trumpet of God' (1 Thess. 4:16).

'The coming of the Lord is at hand' (Jas. 5:8).

'Wait for and hasten the coming of the day of God' (2 Pet. 3:12).

'He who testifies to these things says, "SURELY I AM COMING SOON"' (Rev. 22:20).

* * *

There's a hush of expectation, and a quiet in the air,
And the breath of God is moving in the fervent breath of prayer,
For the eastern skies are glowing as with lights of hidden fire,
And the hearts of men are stirring with the throb of deep desire.

There's a light upon the mountains, and the day is at the spring,
When our eyes shall see the beauty and the glory of the King;
Weary was our heart with waiting, and the night-watch seemed so long,
But His triumph day is breaking, and we hail it with a song!

ANSWER GUIDE

The following pages contain an Answer Guide. It is recommended that answers to the questions be attempted before turning to this guide. It is only a guide and the answers given should not be treated as exhaustive.

GUIDE TO INTRODUCTORY STUDY

The dramatization, 'Paul in Thessalonica', seeks to give a solid background to the Epistles I and 2 Thessalonians. These were real people in a real-life situation. Bring a map with you to the study, if possible.

1. Allocate parts for the play reading. Choose your best reader as Paul. There are 14 characters, but Dan, Reuben, Aristarchus, Secundus and Demas may double with X, Y, City man, Jew I and Jew 2 if necessary.
2. Read the play together as dramatically as possible.
3. Look up Acts 17:1-10 and ask someone to read it aloud.
4. Read the following excerpt from 'The New Bible Dictionary' (IVF):

   'Paul and his companions had to leave Thessalonica hastily in the early summer of AD 50, after making a number of converts and planting a church in the city. The circumstances of their departure meant that their converts would inevitably be exposed to persecution, for which they were imperfectly prepared, because Paul had not had time to give them all the basic teaching which he thought they required. At the earliest opportunity he sent Timothy back to see how the Thessalonian Christians were faring. When Timothy returned to him in Corinth, he brought good news of their steadfastness and zeal in propagating the Gospel, but reported that they had certain problems. Paul was overjoyed at Timothy's good news, and wrote at once to congratulate and encourage his friends, and to deal with their practical problems. The letter which he wrote has come down to us as I Thessalonians.'

5. The books of I and 2 Thessalonians contain much teaching on the return of our Lord Jesus Christ. As we go through the studies, we shall find this subject coming through like a refrain, over and over again. Look up the following references in class to prepare for this

I Thess. 1:10	I Thess. 5:23
I Thess. 2:19-20	2 Thess. 1:7
I Thess. 3:13	2 Thess. 1:10
I Thess. 4:16-18	2 Thess. 2:1

Thessalonians opens up the subject of the return of Christ for further study for those who want to go deeper. The following excerpt from G. T. Manley's book *The Return of Jesus Christ* may clarify the three types of interpretation which are held about the 'thousand years' or MILLENNIUM mentioned in Revelation 20:

> The different views of the time of the Advent in relation to the Millennium have been labelled 'pre-millennial' if the Advent comes before the Millennium, 'post-millennial' if it comes later, and 'a-millennial' if the Millennium is given a purely 'spiritual' meaning unrelated to the Advent.
>
> a. The post-millennial view takes two forms, one looking upon the thousand years as already past, and the other looking for them in the future. Among the former Aquinas saw the fulfilment of the prophecy in the victory of the Catholic Church commencing with the conversion of Constantine; Hengstenberg saw it in the spread of Christianity from the reign of Charlemagne until the French Revolution. The other form of this view expects to see the fulfilment in a great expansion of the visible Church. In the Victorian period it was sometimes combined with an optimism which looked forward to a gradual upward evolution leading to peace and prosperity, and culminating in the Advent of Christ. Of recent years it has been adopted by some liberals who deny any reality to the Advent other than the continual presence of Christ in the Church.
>
> b. The a-millennial view has defenders among both liberals and conservatives. It is upheld in Swete's commentary and is ably expounded by W. Hendriksen in *More than Conquerors* and by W. J. Crier in his small book *The Momentous Event*. The upholders of this view agree with Augustine in 'spiritualizing' the 'first resurrection'; and applying the millennial reign, either to the present experience of Christians, or to the reign of the souls of the martyrs and others in heaven .
>
> c. The pre-millennial view takes many different forms, including that known as 'dispensationalism'. Their common element is the belief that Revelation 20 should be regarded as prophetic of a period of time subsequent to the Advent. The expectation of a millennial reign on earth following Christ's return was the prevailing view of the Christian writers of the first three centuries, and is widely held today.

GUIDE TO STUDY 1

DAY 1

a) The people who have accepted Christ and belong to Him. (Compare this with the present day meaning of the church as being a building.)
b) The Christian is 'in' or 'belonging to' God and the Lord Jesus. This implies the very closest relationship possible.

DAY 2

a) Their work of faith (faith shown in action), labour of love (loving deeds), and steadfastness of hope (steady looking forward to Christ's return.)
b) They remain, abide, last for ever. That God has chosen those who are His. So that His children might be holy and blameless before Him.

DAY 3

a) That God had chosen those who are His.
b) So that His children might be holy and blameless before Him.

DAY 4

a) Paul's and the Lord's.
b) He made their lives an example to others.
c) If we seek to please the Lord, our lives will be a blessing to others.

DAY 5

Personal.

DAY 6

Faith – Turned to God from idols.
Love – Serve the living and true God (or giving Paul a welcome)
Hope – Wait for the return of Jesus from Heaven.

DAY 7

a) A Christian: belongs to God and the Lord Jesus; has faith and shows this in action; works in love; looks forward to Christ's return; is chosen by God; receives the Word by the Holy Spirit; imitates the Lord; witnesses to others; serves God as his Master.
b) Personal.

GUIDE TO STUDY 2

DAY 1 Yes. A life of holiness and godliness (but note: one does not withdraw into a monastery to live this kind of life.)

DAY 2 a) They were dragged bodily to the market place, humiliated, stripped, beaten, thrown into prison with their feet in stocks.
b) God gave them courage; it was beyond human resources.

DAY 3 a) He says he was entrusted with it (v. 4), he does not claim that it was his own, he takes no credit for it. He refers to it as 'The Gospel of God' (vv. 2, 8, 9, etc.)
b) To please God.

DAY 4 a) Gentle, caring and loving. (v. 8. Refer to end of Study 1, 'Love-Self-giving'.)
b) To lead a life worthy of God i.e., to follow more closely the teachings of Jesus, care for others, be joyful, thankful and keep on praying.

DAY 5 a) When the people heard the Word of God, they recognized it as such (compare Day 3).
b) They were persecuted by their own people.

DAY 6 a) To the activity of Satan.
b) He is looking forward to meeting the Lord Jesus in the company of those who have become Christians through his preaching.

DAY 7 a) Verse 2: Faith
Verse 8: Love
Verse 19: Hope
b) Personal.

GUIDE TO STUDY 3

DAY 1
a) Earnest prayer.
b) Personal. Read Romans 8:26-28 in NEB if you can.
Although we often don't know how to pray, we can ask the Holy Spirit to show us.

DAY 2
a) Having no news of whether the Thessalonian Christians were standing firm in the faith or not. Sent Timothy to find out.
b) He warned them that persecution and suffering would come but encouraged them to stand firm.

DAY 3
a) That the Christians at Thessalonica had strong faith (in God) and love (towards men). Also that they longed to see Paul again. (NB. The word used for 'good news' is the one usually translated 'gospel'. This shows that Paul really considered this tremendous news, and it reminded him of the faithfulness and power of God.)
b) Personal.

DAY 4
a) Personal.
b) Personal.

DAY 5
a) He thanked God for them and for the joy they were to him. He prayed night and day for them, and he prayed that God would allow him to see them again.
b) Personal.

DAY 6
a) 1. That God will allow him to visit them again. (Compare with ch. 2:18 – God is stronger than Satan.)
2. That God will increase the love they have for one another.
3. That God will make their hearts strong, sinless and holy.
b) So that we may be able to stand before Him when He returns.

DAY 7
a) For those who have accepted Him as Saviour, and also for all future believers (this includes us).
b) 1. That they may stand firm in the faith (v. 11).
2. That God will keep them from the evil one (v. 15).
3. That God will make them pure and holy.
4. That all believers may be one in Christ.

1 & 2 THESSALONIANS • ANSWER GUIDE

GUIDE TO STUDY 4

DAY 1   a) Four or five times (depending on which version is used).
b) By giving us His Holy Spirit (see I Cor. 6:19).

DAY 2   a) Because God has commanded that we must be holy in order to have fellowship with a holy God.
b) By acknowledging and confessing my sins to God.

DAY 3   Personal.

DAY 4   Sexual purity.

DAY 5   a) God will avenge the wrong done, by punishing the wrongdoer.
b) God. We are implying that we are wiser than He is.

DAY 6   a) To love others more and more.
b) So that unbelievers will trust and respect them; So that they will earn enough to keep themselves. (See 2 Thess. 3:11-12, where some Christians were not working because they expected Christ to return right away).

DAY 7   a) Live a life of holiness and obedience to the Lord.
b) The Lord's return and the end of the age may come at any time and we must be ready .

GUIDE TO STUDY 5

DAY 1
a) They believed Christ would return in their day and when some of their number died they thought they might have missed out. (There may be different answers given which would also be correct. As the answer is not contained in the text refer to Study 5 notes together.)
b) Yes.

DAY 2
a) Because we have the sure and certain hope of resurrection when Christ comes again.
b) Those who have no hope.

DAY 3
a) The resurrection of Jesus.
b) The difference between a seed and a plant.

DAY 4
a) By reminding them that the Bible is the Word of God to us, that accepting it by faith brings peace and Christian growth and by showing that Jesus Himself is Truth.
b) No.

DAY 5
a) The Lord Himself, the Son of Man.
b) Being with the Lord for ever. (Phillips' translation of v. 16 reads, 'One word of command, one shout from the Archangel, one blast from the trumpet of God, and God in person will come down from Heaven!')

DAY 6
a) We have the assurance that the power of God will never be defeated; God is stronger than death.
b) In times of difficulty we can remember that God is over all. When Christian loved ones die we can know that they are safe with Jesus. Though world events trouble us we can remember that in God's good time He will bring this age to its close. In face of death ourselves we can remain calm and triumphant, knowing that life with Christ is everlasting. Personal.

DAY 7
a) That there is a judgment and unbelievers can only expect eternal separation from God.
b) By the absence of things which in this life cause sorrow and suffering. (See also I Cor. 2:9).

GUIDE TO STUDY 6

DAY 1 a) It will be sudden and unexpected.
b) Be ready.

DAY 2 a)

Light	Darkness
day	night
awake	asleep
stay sober	get drunk
all that is good	unfruitful works
visible	secretive
Christ	sin

b) Faith, hope and love.

DAY 3 a) Salvation through Jesus (v. 9); also 2 Peter 3:9.
b) So that we might live with Him.

DAY 4 a) In the previous verses we are exhorted to live as sons of light so that we may be ready to meet Him, and in these verses there is practical advice on how to do this.
b) verses 12, 13 to laymen; verse 14 to leaders.

DAY 5 a)

Positive	Negative
Rejoice	Don't quench the Spirit
Pray	Don't despise prophesying
Give thanks	Abstain from evil
Test everything	
Hold fast what is good	

b) Personal.

DAY 6 a) Personal.
b) Live holy, godly lives.

DAY 7 a) Stand firm against erroneous doctrine.
b) Grow in grace and in the knowledge of our Lord Jesus.

GUIDE TO STUDY 7

DAY 1
a) From the Jews and possibly the city authorities.
b) Their faith has grown, their love for one another has increased and their patience has been evident.

DAY 2
a) To strengthen their faith in God (v. 4) and to mould their characters, making them ready for the Kingdom.
b) Judgment and punishment.

DAY 3
a) 'Those who refuse to acknowledge God and those who will not obey the gospel.' (NEB)
b) It is perfectly in keeping with the character of God. All through the Bible God is shown as righteous and just, as well as loving.

DAY 4
a) Eternal punishment for the ungodly, eternal life in God's presence for His children.
b) verse 41.

DAY 5
a) Either: To be sure we are ready to meet Him or: To be sure we really know Him (v. 12)
b) No.

DAY 6
a) That Jesus is going to return.
b) Exclusion from the presence of the Lord.
Verses 9-10 in J. B. Phillips read, 'Their punishment will be eternal exclusion from the radiance of the Face of the Lord, and the glorious majesty of His power. But to those whom He has made holy, His coming will mean splendour unimaginable. It will be a breathtaking wonder to all who believe.'

DAY 7
a) Personal.
b) The realization that Christ will return to execute judgment as well as to take believers to be with Him prompts Paul to pray that his friends will grow more and more in their faith and in the purpose God has for them.

GUIDE TO STUDY 8

DAY 1 a) That the 'day of the Lord' had already come.
b) Living in idleness, not doing any work. (Did they think there was no need to get a job if Jesus was coming any day?)

DAY 2 a) There will be a time of final rebellion against God. (Note: AV does not give full force to the word 'apostasia' by translating it as 'falling away'.)
b) Wickedness will be revealed in human form (NEB), i.e., The man of lawlessness is revealed (RSV).
c) He will defy every other god or religion there is and will take his seat in the temple of God, claiming to be God.

DAY 3 a) There is a restraining power holding him back until his time comes. (Note: God is the restraining power. He may choose to use human channels e.g., the Roman Empire, the principle of law and government **or spiritual forces, but He is in control and will restrain the Evil One until the time appointed.)**
b) The Lord Jesus will destroy him with the breath of His mouth and annihilate him by the radiance of His coming (v. 8 NEB).

DAY 4 a) The literal translation of verse 9 is 'all power and signs and wonders of lying'. Phillips says, 'all the force, wonders and signs that falsehood can devise.'
b) Those who refused to believe the truth.

DAY 5 a) False prophets. The dragon, that ancient serpent, the deceiver of the whole world, the accuser of the brethren.
b) Christ is stronger than Satan, and will be victorious. Those who endure to the end will be saved. They will conquer Satan by the blood of the Lamb and by the word of their testimony.

DAY 6 a) They are beloved by the Lord and chosen by Him.
b) Stand firm, and keep a strong grip on the truth in God's Word.

DAY 7 a) He loved us, and gave us 'unending encouragement and unfailing hope by His grace.' (Phillips)
b) That God will comfort their hearts, help them in everything they do, make their love grow and overflow, make their hearts strong, sinless and holy (LB). He also prays that the grace, love and fellowship of the Trinity will be with them.

1 & 2 THESSALONIANS · ANSWER GUIDE

GUIDE TO STUDY 9

DAY 1   Personal.

DAY 2   a) Personal (vv. 8, 9).
b) Making the most of the time.

DAY 3   a) Pray for others.
b) That God's Word (through him) may accomplish the glorious work of winning men to Christ, and that he might be protected from evil to continue this work.
Personal.

DAY 4   a) The opportunity to put into practice the things we learn from God's Word.
b) Because God is faithful, He will strengthen us and guard us from the evil one. We have a personal knowledge of the One in whom we put our trust.

DAY 5   a) So that ultimately the disobedient ones would be ashamed of their behaviour and do what was required.
(Leaders may like to refer to I Corinthians 5:1-5. Though this is a difficult passage, it shows the ultimate goal for discipline.)
b) We can treat them with brotherly love.

DAY 6   a) The satisfaction of an honest day's work.
b) They would not 'sponge' on each other, would have money to give to those in need, would occupy their time usefully, etc.

DAY 7   a) Peace with God and the peace of God.
b) Grace and peace (Ib blessing and peace). Personal.

NOTES

OLD TESTAMENT

Triumphs Over Failures: A Study in Judges ISBN 1-85792-888-1 (below left)
Messenger of Love: A Study in Malachi ISBN 1-85792-885-7
The Beginning of Everything: A Study in Genesis 1-11 ISBN 0-90806-728-3
Hypocrisy in Religion: A Study in Amos ISBN 0-90806-706-2
Unshakeable Confidence: A Study in Habakkuk & Joel ISBN 0-90806-751-8
A Saviour is Promised: A Study in Isaiah 1 - 39 ISBN 0-90806-755-0
The Throne and Temple: A Study in 1 & 2 Chronicles ISBN 1-85792-910-1
Our Magnificent God: A Study in Isaiah 40 - 66 ISBN 1-85792-909-8
The Cost of Obedience: A Study in Jeremiah ISBN 0-90806-761-5
Focus on Faith: A Study of 10 Old Testament Characters ISBN 1-85792-890-3
Faith, Courage and Perserverance: A Study in Ezra ISBN 1-85792-949-7

 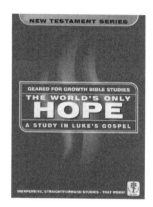

NEW TESTAMENT

The World's Only Hope: A Study in Luke ISBN 1-85792-886-5 (above right)
Walking in Love: A Study in John's Epistles ISBN 1-85792-891-1
Faith that Works: A Study in James ISBN 0-90806-701-1
Made Completely New: A Study in Colossians & Philemon ISBN 0-90806-721-6
Jesus-Christ, Who is He? A Study in John's Gospel ISBN 0-90806-716-X
Entering by Faith: A Study in Hebrews ISBN 1-85792-914-4
Heavenly Living: A Study in Ephesians ISBN 1-85792-911-X
The Early Church: A Study in Acts 1-12 ISBN 0-90806-736-4
The Only Way to be Good: A Study in Romans ISBN 1-85792-950-0

CHARACTERS

Abraham: A Study of Genesis 12-25 ISBN 1-85792-887-3 (below left)
Serving the Lord: A Study of Joshua ISBN 1-85792-889-X
Achieving the Impossible: A Study of Nehemiah ISBN 0-90806-707-0
God plans for Good: A Study of Joseph ISBN 0-90806-700-3
A Man After God's Own Heart: A Study of David ISBN 0-90806-746-1
Grace & Grit: A Study of Ruth & Esther ISBN 1-85792-908-X
Men of Courage: A Study of Elijah & Elisha ISBN 1-85792-913-6
Meek but Mighty: A Study of Moses ISBN 1-85792-951-9

THEMES

God's Heart, My Heart: World Mission ISBN 1-85792-892-X (above right)
Freedom: You Can Find it! ISBN 0-90806-702-X
Freely Forgiven: A Study in Redemption ISBN 0-90806-720-8
The Problems of Life! Is there an Answer? ISBN 1-85792-907-1
Understanding the Way of Salvation ISBN 0-90082-880-3
Saints in Service: 12 Bible Characters ISBN 1-85792-912-8
Finding Christ in the Old Testament: Pre-existence and Prophecy
ISBN 0-90806-739-9

THE WORD WORLDWIDE

We first heard of WORD WORLDWIDE over 20 years ago when Marie Dinnen, its founder, shared excitedly about the wonderful way ministry to one needy woman had exploded to touch many lives. It was great to see the Word of God being made central in the lives of thousands of men and women, then to witness the life-changing results of them applying the Word to their circumstances. Over the years the vision for WORD WORLDWIDE has not dimmed in the hearts of those who are involved in this ministry. God is still at work through His Word and in today's self-seeking society, the Word is even more relevant to those who desire true meaning and purpose in life. WORD WORLDWIDE is a ministry of WEC International, an interdenominational missionary society, whose sole purpose is to see Christ known, loved and worshipped by all, particularly those who have yet to hear of His wonderful name. This ministry is a vital part of our work and we warmly recommend the WORD WORLDWIDE 'Geared for Growth' Bible studies to you. We know that as you study His Word you will be enriched in your personal walk with Christ. It is our hope that as you are blessed through these studies, you will find opportunities to help others discover a personal relationship with Jesus. As a mission we would encourage you to work with us to make Christ known to the ends of the earth.

Stewart and Jean Moulds – British Directors, **WEC International.**

A full list of over 50 'Geared for Growth' studies can be obtained from:

John and Ann Edwards
5 Louvaine Terrace, Hetton-le-Hole, Tyne & Wear, DH5 9PP
Tel. 0191 5262803 Email: rhysjohn.edwards@virgin.net

Anne Jenkins
2 Windermere Road, Carnforth, Lancs., LA5 9AR
Tel. 01524 734797 Email: anne@jenkins.abelgratis.com

UK Website: www.gearedforgrowth.co.uk

Christian Focus Publications

publishes books for all ages

Our mission statement –

STAYING FAITHFUL

In dependence upon God we seek to help make His infallible word, the Bible, relevant. Our aim is to ensure that the Lord Jesus Christ is presented as the only hope to obtain forgiveness of sin, live a useful life and look forward to heaven with Him.

REACHING OUT

Christ's last command requires us to reach out to our world with His gospel. We seek to help fulfil that by publishing books that point people towards Jesus and help them develop a Christ-like maturity. We aim to equip all levels of readers for life, work, ministry and mission.

Books in our adult range are published in three imprints.

Christian Focus contains popular works including biographies, commentaries, basic doctrine, and Christian living. Our children's books are also published in this imprint.

Mentor focuses on books written at a level suitable for Bible College and seminary students, pastors, and other serious readers; the imprint includes commentaries, doctrinal studies, examination of current issues, and church history.

Christian Heritage contains classic writings from the past.

For details of our titles visit us on our website
www.christianfocus.com

Christian Focus Publications, Ltd
Geanies House, Fearn,
Ross-shire, IV20 ITW, Scotland, United Kingdom
info@christianfocus.com